NATURE CLOSE-UP
JUNIORS

Homes

TEXT BY ELAINE PASCOE

PHOTOGRAPHS BY DWIGHT KUHN

BLACKBIRCH PRESS

An imprint of Thomson Gale, a part of The Thomson Corporation

THOMSON

™

GALE

Detroit • New York • San Francisco • San Diego • New Haven, Conn. • Waterville, Maine • London • Munich

For more information, contact
Blackbirch Press
27500 Drake Rd.
Farmington Hills, MI 48331-3535
Or you can visit our Internet site at http://www.gale.com

Photo Credits: All pages © Dwight R. Kuhn Photography

LIBRARY OF CONGRESS CATALOGING-IN-PUBLICATION DATA

Pascoe, Elaine.
Home / text by Elaine Pascoe ; photographs by Dwight Kuhn.
   p. cm. — (Nature close-up junior)
 Includes bibliographical references and index.
 ISBN 1-4103-0313-6 (hardcover : alk. paper)

 1. Household animals—Juvenile literature. 2. Arthropod pests—Juvenile literature. I.
Kuhn, Dwight, ill. II. Title III. Series: Pascoe, Elaine. Nature close-up junior.

 QL49.P25795 2004
 591.75'54—dc22

                                                                                    2004015365

Printed in China
10 9 8 7 6 5 4 3 2 1

Contents

Read this first:

Have fun when you search for wildlife around your home, but be smart. Don't bother the animals that you find—just watch and enjoy them.

Did you know that wild animals may be living in your home? You won't see a bear in your bedroom or a kangaroo in the kitchen. But lots of smaller animals live in and around people's homes. Some of these animals are welcome visitors. Others are pests. But even pests can be fun to watch.

Often people do not know that wildlife shares their homes. But you can find the wildlife. You just have to know where and how to look. Even a city apartment can be a home, or **habitat,** for wildlife.

This house is a home for people—and for wildlife.

Nesting Birds

Some birds build their nests outside of people's homes. Birds called phoebes often do this. Phoebes are named for their call, which sounds like a hoarse "fee-bee."

A pair of phoebes finds a ledge or a nook under the **eaves** of a house. They

A young phoebe peeks out of a nest under the eaves of a house.

build a cup-shaped nest of moss and other plant material, stuck together with bits of mud. Sometimes the birds nest over doorways. They fly around when people go in or out of the door, trying to defend the nest.

Barn swallows live in open country. They like to nest on the rafters of barns or under the eaves of houses. The swallows build nests of mud, straw, and twigs. They line the nests with feathers.

Phoebes and barn swallows are good birds to have around a house. They catch and eat flying insects that can bother people. People often put out nest boxes or shelves for these birds.

Young barn swallows wait for food with open mouths.

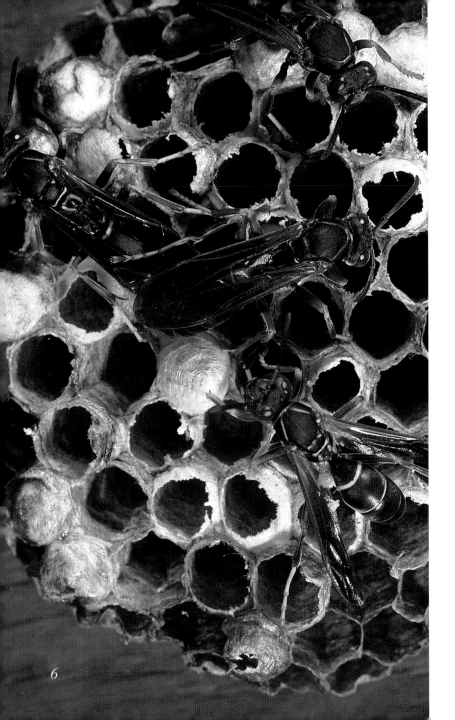

Wasps

Wasps build nests under the eaves of houses, too. Paper wasps make their nests of paper. Just like the paper of this page, the wasps' paper is made from wood pulp. The wasps nibble bits of old wood and plant stems. They chew the bits until they are mashed into wet pulp. Then they add the pulp to the nest in thin layers. The layers dry to form paper.

The nest is made up of lots of little paper cells. The wasp queen lays her eggs in the cells. When the eggs hatch, worker wasps care for the young.

Mud dauber wasps build nests of mud. The female gathers mud and shapes it into tubes. Into each tube she stuffs an insect or spider that she has

Paper wasps build their nest. The queen wasp will lay an egg in each cell.

caught. This **prey** will be food for her young. She lays an egg in each tube. Then she seals the tube and leaves. When the young hatch, they feed on the prey and grow.

They break out of the tube as adult wasps and fly off on their own.

Wasps can sting, so it is best not to bother them. But mud daubers rarely bother people.

Top right: A cutaway view shows prey inside a wood dauber tube. *Top left:* A young wasp grows inside the tube. *Bottom.* A wood wasp carries a caterpillar to a hole in a windowsill. The wasp will lay an egg in the hole. It will seal the caterpillar inside with the egg, as food for the young.

Insect Guests

On summer nights, moths and other insects fly to house lights. You often see them fluttering around porch lights or on window screens. This is a good time for a close look at these insects. You can see their six legs and other body parts.

Ladybugs live near many houses. In fall, you may see groups of ladybugs at your window—or inside your home, on walls or houseplants. The ladybugs squeeze through tiny cracks around windows and doors. They are looking for a warm, safe place to **hibernate** through winter.

Crickets live outside, but they sometimes enter houses in late summer and fall. Crickets are easier to hear than to see. They make chirping noises by rubbing their wings on their hind legs. They hide during the day and are busy at night.

Colorful moths may land on window screens at night.

Ladybugs may try to come indoors in fall.

Keep a Cricket

Look for crickets outside. You may find them where the soil meets the wall of a house, in a garage, or under rocks. If you find one, keep it for a few days to study it.

What to do:
- Put sand in the bottom of the jar. Add a few dry leaves or pieces of bark, to make hiding places for your cricket.
- Put the cricket in the jar. Cover the top with mesh, held on tightly by a rubber band.
- Feed the cricket bits of grass, lettuce, raw potato, fruit, or dog biscuit.
- Give water by misting the inside of the jar daily with a spray bottle. Or soak a cotton ball in water and put it in the jar.

After you have watched the cricket for a day or two, put it back where you found it.

Insect Pests

Many insects are not welcome in homes. They are pests that spoil food, spread dirt, and do damage.

Most ants live in groups, or **colonies**, outside. They may come into houses looking for food. But colonies of carpenter ants sometimes live in the walls of houses. These ants can chew through wood. They may make their nests and tunnels in wooden beams.

Carpenter ants do not eat wood. Termites do. In the forest, they help break down dead trees and fallen branches. But when termites nibble the wood of a house, they do a lot of damage. Like ants, termites live in colonies.

Top: Carpenter ants nest in walls. This ant is carrying a pupa. *Bottom:* Termites damage homes by eating wood.

Cockroaches hide during the day. At night they come out to look for food. These insects eat almost anything. You may see cockroaches at unwashed dishes or pet food bowls. Cockroaches can spread disease.

You may see silverfish in a basement or a bathroom. These insects like damp, cool places. They eat starchy food, like flour and cereal. They also eat paper, fabric, wallpaper paste, and even the glue used in books!

Wash dishes. Clean up spills. Store food carefully. Those steps will help keep pests out of your home.

A cockroach has found food that was left out. *Inset:* A silverfish is an unwelcome guest.

A housefly has huge eyes. Its tongue is like a tube. *Inset:* Housefly pupae.

Fast Fliers

Have you ever tried to swat a housefly? The fly probably darted away. Houseflies are fast fliers. And they have huge **compound eyes.** A fly can see a swat coming from any direction.

A housefly feeds on liquids. Its mouth is a tube, like a straw. At the tip of the tube is a little pad. The pad acts like a sponge to pull in liquids. Because houseflies can spread disease, they are pests.

Houseflies lay their eggs in rotting garbage and other wastes. The young that hatch from the eggs are called maggots. They look like tiny white worms. The maggots feed on the wastes and grow. Then each maggot forms a hard outer case and becomes a **pupa.** Inside its case, it changes. It breaks out of the case as an adult fly.

Pest Taste Test

You may find flour beetles or their young, called mealworms, in a bag of flour or an old box of cereal. You can also buy these insects from pet stores or mail order companies like those on page 24. Do this experiment to see what they like to eat.

like those on page 24.

What to do:

- Place different foods in separate areas of the box. You can use sugar, oatmeal, crushed cereal, flour, or other foods. Add a piece of raw potato to give the insects some moisture.
- Add the mealworms or beetles. Cover the box with mesh, held on with a rubber band.
- Watch to see what the insects eat. Replace the potato every day, as it will dry out.

Spiders

Look in the basement, garage, or under the eaves of a house for cobwebs. The common house spider makes these webs to trap insects.

Like all spiders, the house spider has eight legs. It makes strands of sticky silk that it weaves into its web. An insect that blunders into the web is caught. The spider runs out and bites its prey. The bite injects **venom** that causes the insect to stop moving.

Not all spiders make webs. The jumping spider roams around looking for prey. It jumps to catch its meal.

Many people are afraid of spiders. A few spiders, such as the black widow, have bites that are harmful to people. But most spiders cannot hurt you. By catching insect pests, spiders help people.

The jumping spider looks scary but does not bother people. *Inset:* The bite of the black widow spider can be harmful.

Spider Spotlight

House spiders usually build their webs in dark, out-of-the-way places like basements. Do this activity to see how they act in colored lights.

What to do:
- Find a house spider in its web.
- Turn off the lights, and shine the flashlight on the spider. What does it do?
- Try again with colored light. Put a plastic sheet over the flashlight beam. Watch to see how the spider acts.
- Repeat the activity with different colors. What colors bother the spider most?

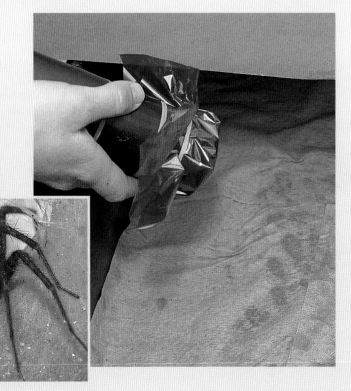

Hunters

Many other animals hunt for insects around people's homes. In the southern United States, you may see an anole lizard at your house. These lizards eat moths, crickets, beetles, flies, and other insects. During the day they like to sunbathe. They stretch out on sunny walkways, window ledges, or garden plants near the warm walls of houses.

Night brings other **predators.** Nighthawks catch flying insects on the wing. During the day these birds may rest quietly on rooftops. With their gray-brown feathers, they are hard to spot.

Left: An anole lizard sunbathes in a garden. *Below:* A nighthawk rests on a house roof.

Bats swoop through the night air in search of insects, too. Bats fly like birds, but they are **mammals.** Up close, they look like mice with wings. During the day, bats rest in hidden places. Sometimes they squeeze through attic vents. The bats hang upside down, wrapped in their wings, until dark. Then they fly out to hunt.

A bat finds its way with a sort of radar. The bat sends out high-pitched sounds. The sounds bounce off other objects, creating echoes. The echoes tell the bat what is out there in the dark.

Bats scare some people. But they are not harmful. They help by catching bothersome insects.

A brown bat hangs upside down in an attic. After dark, it will fly out to hunt for insects.

17

Too Small to See

Some of the wildlife in your home may be too small to see. Tiny dust mites live in bedding, couches, and carpets—even in stuffed toys! They are related to spiders. Dust mites eat tiny bits of dead skin that fall from people and pets.

Mold **spores** float through the air. If a mold spore lands in the right spot, mold begins to grow. There are many kinds of mold. Most kinds prefer damp, dark places. Some kinds grow on food.

You need a microscope to see dust mites and mold spores. But even if you cannot see them, you may know they are around. These tiny living things make many people sneeze and cough.

Tiny specks of dark mold grow on this bread.

Molds on Food

Which foods will molds grow best on? Make your best guess. Then do this experiment to find out.

What You Need:
- Disposable container
- Paper towel
- Pieces of different foods
- Plastic wrap
- Rubber band

What to do:
- Moisten a paper towel. Put it in the bottom of the container.
- Put bits of different foods on the paper towel. You can use pieces of fruit, bread, and other food.
- Leave the container uncovered for about 30 minutes. Mold spores will fall in it, though you will not see them. Then cover the container with plastic wrap, held on by a rubber band.
- Put the container in a warm place. Check every day or so for mold. Which foods grow the most mold?
- Do not open the container. Throw it away when you are done.

Furry Visitors

Mice come to people's homes looking for food scraps. They may nest in a garage or even in the walls of a house. Like all mammals, a female mouse feeds her young with milk that her body produces.

You may see other mammals around your home. Squirrels come looking for seeds and nuts. They are fun to watch as they climb and leap. In winter squirrels sometimes nest in attics. Like mice, they make a mess–so they are not welcome inside.

Raccoons are nighttime visitors. With their black masks, they look like bandits. They act like bandits, too. They raid bird feeders, pet food bowls, and garbage cans. During the day raccoons rest, usually in hollow trees. But a raccoon may curl up under a porch or deck, or even climb into an attic!

Left: A white-footed mouse cares for her young in a nest in a garage.
Right: A raccoon raids a garbage can.

Home Wildlife Hunt

Go on a hunt for wildlife in your home. Make a nature notebook to record your finds.

What You Need:

- Notebook
- Pencil
- Hand lens

What to do:

- Look around your house for wildlife—flies, spiders, and other creatures. When you find an animal, study it closely. A hand lens will help.
- Make a chart in your notebook, and write down information about it: How big is it? How does it move? How fast is it? How many legs does it have? Include a drawing of the creature.
- Try to identify the animal. Compare it to pictures in books and on Web sites, such as those on page 24.

Animal — Housefly

How many legs — 6

Does it have wings — yes

How does it move —

Where was it found —

Words to Know

colonies: groups of living things, all of the same kind

compound eyes: eyes with many lenses. Such eyes are good for seeing motion.

eaves: the underside of an overhanging roof

habitat: the place where a plant or animal naturally lives

hibernate: to rest in a deep sleep in which heart rate, breathing, and other body functions slow down

mammals: animals that have fur, give birth to live young, and nurse their young with milk

predators: animals that kill and eat other animals

prey: animals that are hunted by predators

pupa: a stage in an insect's life during which it changes into an adult

spores: special cells that can grow into a living thing, such as a mold

venom: poison

For More Information

Books

Eleanor Christian, et al., *Looking at Ants.* Mankato, MN: Pebble Books, 2000.

Ann Earle, *Zipping, Zapping, Zooming Bats.* New York: HarperTrophy, 1995.

Allan Fowler, *Of Mice and Rats.* Danbury, CT: Childrens, 1999.

John Latimer and Karen Stray Noling, *Backyard Birds.* Boston: Houghton Mifflin, 1999.

Carolyn B. Otto, *Spiders.* New York: Scholastic, 2002.

Matthew Reinhart, *Young Naturalist's Handbook: Insect-lo-pedia.* New York: Hyperion, 2003.

Websites

Backyard Wildlife Habitat (www.backyardwildlifehabitat.info/kidsnhabitats.htm).
Go on a spider safari and try other fun activities.

eNature.com (www.eNature.com).
This site has field guides that will help you identify wildlife around your home.

Sources

Sources for mealworms or flour beetles:

Carolina Biological Supply Company
2700 York Road
Burlington, NC 27215
(800) 334-5551
www.carosci.com

Connecticut Valley Biological Supply
82 Valley Road, PO Box 326
Southampton, MA 01073
(800) 628-7748
www.ctvalleybio.com

Index

ML   6/08